Self-Confidence

I0410336

How to Be Confident and Improve Your Self-Image

Katy Richards

Table of Contents

Introduction

This book contains proven steps and strategies on how to be confident and improve your self-image.

It is for anyone who is looking for practical steps on how to become confident. It is also for those who want to know more about themselves for self-improvement.

In this book, you will discover all the essential tips you need to become confident enough to overcome the challenges in your life and chase after your goals. Find out what confidence means and the qualities you will find in a confident person. Determine your current level of confidence and learn how you can achieve balance in the different aspects of your life.

Most importantly, you will learn how you can improve your confidence through various strategies. These range from changing your mindset to keeping the right habits, and so much more.

With the help of this book, you can gain the confidence that you need to start building the life that you love. Turn to Chapter 1 and get started now!

Thanks again for downloading this book, I hope you enjoy it!

Chapter 1 – What Confidence is All About?

Hello there! I would like to congratulate you for taking your first step towards becoming a more confident person. You will be glad to know that this adventure will change your life forever.

In this chapter, you will learn about the meaning of confidence. Specifically, you will learn exactly how it is defined and how you can measure your current level of self-confidence. After that, you will learn about the qualities that make a person self-confident. Altogether, you can create a special program to help you gain self-confidence.

Now, without further ado, let's get started!

The Definition of Confidence

First, let's talk about what confidence really is. Some may think that you are born with it and that somehow, parents have this "confidence" gene that gets passed down. Others believe that confidence is more of a skill that can be honed. However, to people who constantly struggle with it, they sometimes see it as a sort of magical elixir that they can drink up to feel super.

In truth, confidence has many meanings. In fact, the dictionary offers not one but **five** meanings of confidence. It is...

1. Believing in yourself and your abilities; a freedom from doubt.

   Sarah was confident that she can do well in the competition for she had trained for it relentlessly in the past 9 months.

2. Trusting in someone or something (which includes yourself).

   The boardroom was in high spirits because Peter has confidence in his partner to make the presentation a success.

3. A feeling of hopefulness that things will come your way.

   Most brides feel nervous before a wedding, but Jessy is confident that hers will be okay because she isn't the type who sweats the small stuff.

4. In the form of a trustful relationship.

   Greta took Simon into his confidence after she found out that he had been secretly helping her all along.

5. A secret that is shared and entrusted to someone.

   Felicity is well-loved for being a dependable friend that is why Tristan always trusted her with his confidence.

Does your perception of confidence fall under any of these five definitions? If not, what do *you* think it means?

With these five definitions in mind, you can easily spot that confidence is not something, which makes you "feel good." Rather, it is mainly about belief, assurance, hopefulness and trust. In a nutshell, this is how we can define it:

Confidence is believing in your ability to make the right decision and take the right steps in a given situation, no matter how difficult or easy it seems to be.

Of course, by having the confidence to overcome life's challenges, there is nothing wrong with feeling good about it. You can even think of it as a positive side effect.

How to Measure your Level of Confidence

If you want to know your current level of confidence, perhaps you would like to take this short test. It will be a great idea to write down your responses in a journal. That way, you can take a look at it later on in the future and see how you have developed since then.

Before you begin, keep in mind that there is no such thing as a right or wrong response. Be honest with yourself as you can then reveal the aspects of your life with an impact on your self-confidence.

Now, keep in mind the following scale:

- Strongly Agree: SA

- Agree: A

- Neutral: N

- Disagree: D

- Strongly Disagree: SD

Write down your response using this guide as you go through each of the following statements:

1. I know exactly how I want to live my life.

2. I know my values clearly.

3. I have chosen a purpose in my life and I am working towards it.

4. I can take a step back to assess my thoughts and emotions during a stressful situation.

5. I do not remind myself constantly of my failures.

6. I have a reputation of being an optimist.

7. I spend most of my time doing the things that I love.

8. I occasionally find myself being incredibly focused on a task.

9. I value myself and the people around me.

10. I am fully aware of both my strengths and flaws.

11. I know what other people see in me.

12. I have no problems with getting into the details and looking at the bigger picture at the same time.

13. I sometimes seek advice from the people I trust when I have decisions to make.

14. I love experiencing new things and I see challenges as an opportunity to grow.

15. I enjoy learning a new skill and opening up to different perspectives.

16. I am willing to take risks in a healthy way.

17. I consider myself as healthy because I take care of my body.

18. I always find time to rest and relax each day.

19. I believe that progress, no matter how small, is better than perfection.

20. I occasionally spend time to concentrate deeply and connect with the different facets of myself.

After responding to each statement, the next step is to score yourself.

- For each "SA" give yourself 5 points.

- For each "A" give yourself 4 points.

- For each "N" give yourself 3 points.

- For each "D" give yourself 2 points.

- For each "SD" give yourself 1 point.

Once you have given yourself the appropriate points for each statement, total your score and compare it with the following rating scale:

If you scored between an 80 and 100:

Overall, you are what others consider as a confident person. You know exactly who you are and what you stand for, and you are currently working towards achieving your goals and purpose in life.

If you scored between a 60 and 79:

You are fairly confident most of the time. There are certain times in your life when you feel challenged, but you know how to manage them by seeking help. You even picked up this book to help you work towards becoming more confident, so good for you!

If you scored between a 40 and 59:

You may be experiencing some doubts in your life as of the moment, and you may be wondering what to do next. Don't worry, because this book is here to help you out! Take as much time as you need to improve yourself and you will soon find yourself impressed with your own progress.

If you scored between a 20 and 39:

Your honesty is something to be admired! While your confidence may not be at a scale that you would prefer, you must know that you have the power to elevate it. You can find all the help you need in this book. Much excitement awaits you because you are about to transform your life for the better.

Now that you know what your current level of confidence is, the next step is to take a look at any of the areas that you strongly agreed and disagreed with. These reveal much of who you are.

For instance, if you strongly disagreed with 13, then it probably means you often feel isolated from others. Perhaps you should spend more time with good friends who can give you a fresh perspective.

And let's say you strongly agreed with 11, then it means you are sensitive and aware towards other people's perception of you. This is a strength just as long as you pay more attention to the positive and constructive side of it.

Overall, these highlights can help you tailor-fit a program, which is most suitable for your needs.

In the next section, you will get to know the qualities of a self-confident person. However, treat it as more of a guide than a cookie cutter image of perfection.

Keep in mind that everyone can harness the qualities of a self-confident person. And while any of these qualities may ebb and flow throughout life, it always helps to stay grounded by knowing the type of person you want to become.

The Qualities of a Self-Confident Person

Have you ever tried something new and challenging, solved a problem, or demonstrated a skill? Did you go through with it even if you did not feel like it? Have you noticed that it wasn't actually *that* bad once you got to do it?

If you did, then your "it wasn't so bad" moment was actually a manifestation of confidence! It is getting out of your comfort zone to achieve something, and no matter how pressured it may have made you feel, you were able to do it.

When you are a self-confident person, you do not mind the feeling of discomfort that a new experience causes. That's because you believe in your ability to overcome it and achieve your goal. When you are confident, you inspire those around you to stop panicking and start taking action.

Now you may think that this is obviously easier said than done. How can you possibly not mind the discomfort when your heart starts to race and you break into a cold sweat?

Well, confident people started out that way, too. However, because they **choose** to believe in themselves, they learn to handle things with poise. Their breath is calm and steady rather than fast and short. Their mindset is all about being proactive and positive, instead of defensive and self-defeating.

To help you have a clearer picture of how to become more self-confident, here are the ten core qualities that will make you one:

1. A positive mindset

You know that there is always a good side in every story. You regard yourself in a positive light and you seek to see the good in others as well.

2. A sense of purpose

You have chosen or even carved your own path in life. You make all the different parts of who you are work together to achieve this purpose.

3. Good health

You respect and therefore care for your body and mind. You believe that your energy impacts your mood. This is why you make sure to nourish your body and give yourself time to rest and relax each day.

4. Emotional stability

You know that the best way to deal with a stressful situation is to stay calm and reasonable. You become aware when you start to feel strong emotions, specifically anxiety, sadness and anger, but you know how to respond to them well.

5. Motivation

You find ways to make your everyday tasks enjoyable, no matter how simple some may seem to be. You know how to focus and get into a "state of flow," or concentrate so well that nothing can distract you.

6. A desire to learn

You take pleasure in learning and experiencing something new. You see each day as an opportunity to develop yourself and you feel grateful for that. You never see yourself as an expert, but as a constant learner.

7. Open-mindedness

Along with the desire to learn, you can also broaden your perspective. You know how to look at a situation from different angles. You can adjust your behavior depending on the circumstances, because you accept diversity.

8. An openness to taking risks.

You can make quick but smart decisions when faced with an uncertain future. You are willing to bet on yourself even if you are still in the process of learning something, because you believe in your ability to manage it.

9. Values and principles.

You know exactly what you want in life and how you want to become. You are fully aware of what is meaningful and important to you, and you stand by what you believe in.

10. **Self-awareness**.

You know your strengths and the qualities that you are still working towards improving. You accept your own individuality and you are okay with your flaws because you also have much more to be proud of yourself.

These may seem like a lot of qualities, but if you stop to think about it, you already possess many them. All you have to do now is to tap the others. By opening yourself up to learning and embracing each of them, you are already on your way to becoming self-confident.

How are you coming along so far? I hope this chapter has helped you shape your own definition of confidence.

At this point, you are ready to take a good look at each aspect of your life and improve on the areas that will help you trust and believe in yourself more. The next chapter, in particular, will discuss the foundation of self-confidence - your mind.

Chapter 2 – It Starts in the Mind

Did you know that some of the most conventionally attractive people in the world also tend to be the most insecure? That's because confidence depends more on your state of mind than appearance.

How do you train your mind to become more confident? Below are several strategies that you can apply. Do your best to go through each one of them and take note of all your insights in your journal.

Reflecting on these insights will help you develop your self-awareness and make you become more sensitive towards your own thoughts and actions. After all, the deeper you get to know your mind, the more responsible you will feel for the choices that you make in life.

Reflect on Past Experiences

You may think that you are the sum of all your experiences in life, but that does not mean you should let that dictate your future. Past experiences are there for you to learn from, however, many people choose to let these define them. What is worse, they have become so attached to their past that it holds them back from unleashing their full potential. Often, people allow their past to dictate their thoughts and behavior because they are unaware of their influence.

For instance, let's say you didn't get good grades in math back when you were in high school. You've associated the subject with negative feelings because of that. It was made worse by a teacher who criticized you harshly in front of the class for it. To make matters worse, your classmates teased you.

Now fast forward to the future. If you are someone with low self-confidence, you will still be holding that imaginary label on your forehead that says "I'm no good at math." Then, every time you are faced with a problem that has to do with numbers, you will immediately give up on yourself. You even have this automatic reaction wherein you say, "Oh, I *can't* do this. I'm bad at math!"

However, if you give yourself some time to reflect and ask yourself *why* you feel this way, then you can overcome it and let go of this imaginary label. You will realize that maybe you just didn't do so well in school because you just didn't spend enough time studying it, or maybe you did but you weren't able to ask someone for guidance.

This leads to a realization that you can be good at math if you want to. After all, you can now find a lot of available resources that you can access to improve this skill. The best part is that there's no mean teacher to embarrass you in front of the class, and no teasing from your classmates to make you feel bad.

As you can see, reflecting on your own reactions to challenging experiences can help you overcome the negativity from your past.

Here are some steps that you can follow to help you overcome setbacks triggered by your past:

Step 1: Go somewhere comfortable and quiet where you won't be disturbed by anyone.

Bring your journal and a pen with you.

Step 2: Close your eyes and try to recall the last time you faced a challenging situation. Let the memory be as vivid as possible. Describe the memory in writing.

For example: *Two weeks ago, my boss told me that I would have to be the one to present the proposal at the meeting. I was only given a week to prepare.*

Step 3: Recall how you reacted to the situation. Try to remember how you thought as well as what you did and say. Capture this memory and put it into writing.

For example: *I felt stressed out and scared. I felt insecure about my presentation skills and I feared that I would embarrass myself in front of everyone. I hated my boss for putting me in such a difficult situation.*

Step 4: Ask yourself: "Why am I reacting this way?"

What event in your past triggers you to feel so negatively about the present situation? Take note of everything that comes to mind.

For example: *Presenting in front of others makes me feel bad because of what happened to me in college a few years ago. I was assigned to present some facts about a subject, but they were inconsistent. Someone criticized me and call me stupid in front of my classmates. I felt like I wanted the ground to open up and swallow me whole.*

Step 5: Ask yourself: "What will I choose to do this time?"

Remember that your negative experience in the past is not the same as what you are facing. While the scenarios have some similarities, the biggest difference now is what you choose to do.

Through these steps, you can detach your past from your present mindset. You are shifting your focus from what went wrong to what you want to transpire. Practicing this exercise will also help you develop self-awareness and enable you to be more open to taking risks, two important qualities that make up self-confidence.

Let Go of the Habit of Making Assumptions

Let's say you woke up one morning and found out that you failed an important test, or that your favorite athlete lost the final match. You think, "Oh man, this day is not going to be a good one." Then, for the rest of the day, you notice every little mistake you make and realize that hey, you're right. It isn't a great day.

The truth is, you only noticed all the negative things that happened during that day because you *chose* it. It all started with the assumption that it wasn't going to be a good day. By making these assumptions, you actually held yourself back from being self-confident that day.

Here are some more statements of people who have the habit of making assumptions. Notice whether you find yourself sounding like them as well:

"She's rich and famous, that's why it's easy for her to be confident."

"I'm never going to be confident enough because I don't have the right skills for the job."

"I think my co-workers don't like me very much. No wonder I'm never confident during meetings."

"My friends are more attractive and talented than me, that's why I can never gain the confidence I need."

What do you think about these assumptions? Can you say that these are unfair? If you find yourself thinking this way, it is important to remind yourself that such thoughts are not based on facts but mere assumptions. They are poisonous because they affect how you think and behave.

The only way to let go of a bad habit such as this one is to replace it with a good one. In this particular case, you can replace your assumptions with an affirmation.

An effective strategy that will help you overcome your assumptions with affirmations is by creating a "But" Sheet. Find out how it works by trying it right now:

Step 1: Divide a sheet of paper into two columns. In the first column, write down the negative assumptions that you have that are affecting your self-confidence.

For example:

- *I'm bad at math because I failed several times during high school.*

- *I could never date anyone because I'm not attractive.*

- *People always stare at me because I'm overweight.*

- *I'm never confident during presentations because they will notice my acne.*

Step 2: Now, in the line between the first and second column, write the word "BUT."

Step 3: Write an affirmation as a response to each of your assumptions, using "but" to connect them.

For example:

- *I'm bad at math because I failed several times during high school BUT I can start learning now!*

- *I could never date anyone because I'm not attractive BUT I still feel and look beautiful because I am healthy.*

- *People always stare at me because I'm overweight BUT I don't care what they think*

> *because I'm taking steps towards improving my health.*

- *I'm never confident during presentations because they will notice my acne BUT I will definitely impress them by practicing and preparing hard.*

By creating these affirmations, you are defeating your assumptions and encouraging yourself to take action towards self-improvement. At first, you will notice that your negative assumptions will be automatic. This is normal, because your mind has gotten used to them. However, by using the trigger word "BUT", you are unlocking your affirmation.

The more often you apply this strategy, the sooner you will notice yourself letting go of making assumptions. Eventually, the negative voice inside your mind, which keeps on making those assumptions will transform into a clever, positive, and problem-solving coach.

Develop an Optimistic Mindset

Optimism is a choice. The more often you choose it, the more naturally it comes. There is nothing to lose and everything to gain, including self-confidence, when you become an optimist.

Optimism is best described as a general disposition, which allows you to expect the best in all things. It means taking responsibility for both your thoughts and actions, and deciding to solve the problem, instead of letting it consume you.

Optimists generally live longer lives than others because they are not as susceptible to anxiety, depression and stress. Their immune system tends to be stronger because of this, and because they take better care of themselves. Moreover, they are faster learners because they are confident in their abilities. On top of that, people just gravitate towards them because they are inspiring, uplifting, and have an overall positive energy about them.

Confident people are optimists, and vice versa. You can even go so far as to say that one cannot be without the other. To gain self-confidence through optimism, here are the steps that you can take right away:

Step 1: Write in a journal each day.

Journaling will literally cause you to face your thoughts on paper. It allows you to not only express yourself better but also monitor the thought patterns that you consistently have. It helps you to take a step back and evaluate the nature of your thoughts.

Try journaling for a week, at least. By the end of the week, read all your entries and ask yourself, "Do I tend to write about positive experiences, or negative ones?"

Step 2: Dispute the negative voice in your mind.

As mentioned in the previous section, negative thoughts tend to be automatic. Now the only way to replace them with positive thoughts is to acknowledge then dispute them.

Aside from the "But" and affirmations strategy, another clever way to respond to negative thoughts is to tune into your logical side. As soon as you start thinking negatively, you stop, think and evaluate it. Ask yourself: Is this based on fact? Is it accurate? Or, am I generalizing? Am I overreacting?

For example, let's say you failed a job interview. Then, a negative thought such as "I'm never going to get a job" pops in your head. As soon as this happens, acknowledge it by saying, "that was a negative thought."

Then, ask yourself, "Is this based on fact, or am I just exaggerating?" Logic will soon follow that you are simply exaggerating because there are still plenty of other opportunities out there that you have not tapped. If you have, then it simply means you need to improve your qualifications. It's not an "all or nothing" scenario.

Step 3: Let go of anything, which contributes to your negative thoughts when you can.

Whether you are aware of it or not, your thoughts are influenced by what surrounds you and by the people you interact with each day.

For instance, if you are fond of watching reality TV shows wherein the participants constantly bicker and fight, you would not be surprised to find yourself feeling easily irritable over small things as well.

To find out what causes you to think negatively about your surroundings, reflect on where you dedicate most of your time each day. Do you read too many gossip magazines? Or do you have lunch each day with a co-worker who always manages to find a problem in every situation?

After pinpointing these sources of negativity, gradually remove them from your life, then replace them with things that will promote positive thinking.

For example, instead of spending time online reading gossip websites, clear your history and bookmark links to inspiring and motivational web pages on your browser.

Now that you have learned the different ways on how to promote a positive and confident mindset, you can now incorporate them into your daily life. Developing an optimistic and confident mindset takes time, so gently remind yourself to practice each day.

Chapter 3 – What you See Affects How you Feel

Do you believe that your physical appearance affects your confidence? Or do you think it is the other way around?

Regardless of how you see it, it is no secret that we humans rely deeply on our sense of sight. This is why one's looks matter in many of life's situations. Your appearance is your physical representation in the world and it communicates a strong message to who you are and what you believe in.

While there is nothing wrong with finding confidence in how you look, it becomes a problem if you compare yourself with others. Insecurities come from using your physical appearance as a measurement of your self-worth.

Instead of focusing on physical appearance to make you feel good, it is important to focus on becoming more confident in your own uniqueness. Keep in mind that confidence in itself will affect how you look and feel in a good way.

If you want to know how to feel more confident in how you look, here are simple yet effective tips that you can apply:

Acknowledge your insecurities to accept them

Our own negative perception of our physical appearance stems from irrational thought. This is why it is important to determine the root cause of what is eating your self-confidence as far as your looks are concerned. That way, we can figure out healthy solutions to overcome these insecurities.

Start by asking yourself, "Why don't I feel confident in how I look?" Write or sketch out any of the thoughts that come to mind.

Then, ask yourself, "Why don't I like these attributes?" and "When did I start to not like them?" Keep writing down everything that comes to mind.

For example: *I don't like myself because of my acne. I think people always stare at me because of how bad my acne is. It all began when I heard someone make a joke about it and everyone laughed.*

After acknowledging these thoughts, the next and most important step is to assure yourself by saying, "I am worth more than how I look. It is merely only a part of a much bigger whole." Remind yourself that everyone, including you, has strengths as well as flaws.

While you are indeed in the process of self-improvement, it does not mean you should simply focus on fixing your flaws. Rather, it is about embracing your strengths and accepting your weaknesses.

Highlight your "assets"

As mentioned earlier, learning to appreciate yourself starts with identifying your "assets." Often, people focus too much on their flaws when they also have something to be proud of about themselves. Since this topic is about physical appearance, you can also identify your physical attributes that make you feel confident in yourself.

Try to recall the times when someone gave you a compliment about how you look. This will help you appreciate more what you already have then go ahead and highlight these attributes.

For instance, someone might have mentioned that you have attractive eyes. If so, then go ahead and let them be the focal point on your face, such as by making better eye contact during your conversations.

Or maybe you were praised for your amazing smile. If so, then greet others with it. In fact, the act of smiling alone can instantly boost your mood.

Be mindful of your posture.

Good posture instantly makes you look and feel more attractive. It makes you appear confident, dependable and strong, all of which are qualities that send positive vibes. No matter how bad your day is, try correcting your slouch and you will instantly notice a change in your mood.

To help you start the habit of maintaining good posture, you should highly consider signing up for flexibility classes. Pilates and yoga, for instance, can do wonders not only to your health and posture, but also to your self-confidence. Give them a try to find out why.

Exercise regularly

It cannot be stressed enough how important exercise is to your physical and mental health. Aside from strengthening your muscles and bones, it also reduces your risk of developing cardiovascular disease. It even lowers symptoms related to anxiety and depression.

If you have never really been fond of exercising, then maybe you just haven't discovered yet the kind, which suits your preference. Nowadays, there are plenty of workout programs to choose from.

Some even do a variety of them to stay motivated and interested. There are also other forms of physical activity that are not called "exercise" but which have the same benefits as well. For instance, gardening and even doing household chores causes you to sweat and move around a lot.

Follow a healthy diet

Many people take for granted the kinds of food they choose to eat. However, the quality of food you consume impacts your physical appearance more than you think.

For instance, healthy foods can naturally make your skin clearer and healthier, and your hair stronger and more vibrant. It will also improve your mood and energy levels, thereby allowing you to feel good as well.

Practice good grooming

Imagine what a smart haircut, an invigorating bath, and crisp, clean clothes can do to anyone. Granted, grooming is the easiest strategy you can employ to instantly improve your physical appearance and self-confidence. While it alone will not solve all your problems, it never hurts to do things with style.

However you want to improve your physical appearance, just remember to always be kind to yourself. Continue to stay positive and be your own cheerleader as you journey on towards self-improvement. For instance, don't beat yourself up for overindulging on chocolate cake at a party when you are on a healthy diet. Just forgive yourself and commit to going back on track.

It is also important to prioritize your health above anything else. You will be amazed how getting enough sleep and letting go of habits such as smoking and drinking too much alcohol can positively affect your self-image. That's because being healthy makes it natural for you to look and feel more attractive and confident.

Chapter 4 – Tap Into your Inner Confidence

Everyone, yourself included, has experienced the feeling of being highly energetic, brave and empowered at certain points in their life. It doesn't matter if you cannot completely recall that moment right now, because what matters more is that you can experience it again.

If you want to know how to tap into your inner confidence, here are effective strategies that you can apply right now:

Capture your Moments of Glory

Reminding yourself of happy times in your life will draw out the confidence trapped inside you. Moreover, recalling them will encourage you to never give up, because it sends a message to yourself that you are capable of doing great things.

Right now, try the following exercises to help you "capture" these moments of glory:

Step 1: Cut out small sheets of paper, about one by three inches each. Make as many pieces as you like, starting with at least ten. You can skip this part if you already have small notepads.

Step 2: Grab a Mason jar or small fish bowl and set aside.

Step 3: On each sheet of paper, write down a memory of a time when you felt proud of an accomplishment. It doesn't matter how big or small it is; what's important is that it makes you feel good.

Step 4: After writing as many of these memories as you can, fold each of them up and place them in your jar or bowl.

Step 5: Place the extra sheets of blank paper and a pen next to it. Every time you experience another "moment of glory," write it down and add it to the jar or bowl.

Keep this nearby and within sight so that you will not forget your little collection. That way, you can easily fish out and read a "moment of glory" in your life whenever you need it.

Manage your Worries

It is natural to feel worries for good reason. For instance, getting worried about a family member who hasn't come home yet within the expected time is within reason. This "fear" will compel you to take immediate action, such as by calling the authorities.

However, entertaining unreasonable, worrisome thoughts will trap you in your own fear, and anxiety will keep you from taking charge of your life. Worrying about things that are no longer within your control, such as the anxiety you feel while waiting for exam results, will eat away your self-confidence and paralyze you.

Fortunately, there are plenty ways to manage your worries and fears so that you can believe in yourself and in others more. One of them is this exercise you can try right now:

Step 1: Ask yourself: "What's making me feel so worried?"

Be as specific as possible so that you can acknowledge and face your fear. This will turn the abstract thought into a problem that you can solve.

Step 2: Recall when you started to feel worried about this.

Determine the root cause of your fear and consider why it still haunts you today.

Step 3: Ask yourself: "Can I do something about it?"

If you do, then immediately write down steps to take to solve the problem. If it is beyond your control, turn your attention to something more productive.

Step 4: Create an action plan that you will follow should you start to worry about it again.

It's natural to feel worried again about something that you already know you should not worry about. However, this time, you'll know how to respond because of your action plan.

Worries can get out of control unless you turn on rational thought. It helps to imagine yourself as a scientist who is observing your worries from a third-person perspective. That way, you will take actionable steps towards a resolution.

Let go of habits that destroy self-confidence

Certain mental habits will keep you from tapping into your self-confidence. Find out what they are so you can gently release them from your thoughts.

1. **Polarizing**

This type of negative thinking pattern is when a person does not believe in a gray area. Perfectionists tend to fall in this "all or nothing" category, which is why they often find it difficult to cope with failure.

How to overcome it: Acknowledge the fact that the gray area does exist. Life is more than just zero and hundred percent, because there is an infinite number of percentages in between.

2. Filtering

When given a compliment and some constructive criticisms, the chance that a pessimist will only focus on the negative comments is high. For instance, if someone told them that they are talented but lazy, they will only beat themselves up for being called lazy. The "talented" part often fails to be acknowledged.

How to overcome it: While it may be automatic for you to instantly zero in on the negative side of things, you can still respond by asking yourself: "What can I learn from this experience?" This will immediately trigger your brain to recognize the compliments you have received and the advice that you can use for self-improvement.

3. Personalizing

People who take things too personally have the habit of making the assumption that when something goes bad, the others will blame them. It is debilitating to have this thought pattern because it prevents you from taking risks and having healthy relationships with others.

How to overcome it: Remind yourself that the world does not revolve around you. For instance, just because someone did not call you up does not mean you are no longer important to him. Instead of obsessing over your assumptions, focus on something productive. In time, the truth will be revealed without you having to worry about it.

4. Catastrophizing

When facing a challenging situation, do you often assume that the worst case scenario is inevitable? If yes, then you have the habit of catastrophizing. Such a thought pattern instantly elevates your stress levels and anxiety, which is why you need to overcome it right away.

How to overcome it: Whenever you start to jump to a negative conclusion, keep in mind that such a thought is neither realistic nor helpful to you. Instead, breathe in deeply to calm yourself down, then ground yourself to the present moment. Focus on the best possible path to take in dealing with the problem before you. Do not try to predict a future, which does not even exist yet.

Always remember you already have a lot of confidence inside you. All you need to do is find a way to tap into it. Whenever you find yourself feeling low and unsure of yourself, gently remind yourself of these simple strategies to boost your self-image instantly and make everything feel right again.

Chapter 5 – Develop Self-Confidence in a Social World

Self-confidence plays a key role in developing your social skills. When you believe in yourself, you can broaden your social circles, advance in your career, and develop meaningful relationships. Confidence also enables you to protect yourself against those who may hurt and take advantage of you. It also keeps you from developing social anxiety and depression.

How do you develop confidence in a world teeming with different people? Here are the fundamental strategies to practice constantly:

Reflect on your existing social skills

Consider how you normally interact with others. If you discover a few trouble spots, then you work towards improving these areas. Here are some questions you can answer to help you know where to get started:

1. Do you tend to slouch when in front of others?

2. Do you keep your head down while talking to someone?

3. Is your voice too loud or too timid?

4. Do you cross your arms or legs when someone is talking to you?

5. Do you smile and make eye contact when someone greets you?

Make eye contact and smile

Do you know what will make the best first impression? Looking at a person's eyes and smiling at him. Not doing so will cause the other person to think that you are insecure, snobbish or not to be trusted.

As soon as you are introduced to someone, do not be shy to smile and make eye contact as you listen to him. Make sure that it is natural instead of "rehearsed," for obvious reasons. If you think you need more practice, try it out with a friend so that you won't feel so self-conscious since you already know each other. Once you get the hang of it, start with the first person to whom you are introduced.

Be a great listener

A healthy dose of self-confidence is great, but too much of it will cause others to walk in the opposite direction as soon as you enter the room. Now, the best way to achieve balance and gain just the right amount of confidence is to develop curiosity towards others – not in an obsessive way, obviously, but in a way that will enable you to actually listen to them.

Better yet, ask follow-up questions so that you can keep the conversation going. For instance, if someone mentioned that they love playing video games, you can ask them which ones they like best. It may sound simple, but it is actually a great technique for those who are still working on building their confidence, because it lets them talk to others without actually being in the spotlight.

Practice confident body language skills

There are books dedicated to helping you improve your body language, especially in a social setting. However, of all the advice you can get, the most basic one to keep in mind is to maintain good posture. It is important to strike that balance that will keep you from looking insecure or arrogant.

The ability to communicate well with others will improve your quality of life in all aspects. Now you may think that developing these social skills requires a lot of confidence, but in reality, you can actually "fake it 'til you make it."

Each day presents to you many social opportunities to pretend as if you are already the most confident that you want to be. Keep in mind that even something as simple as smiling and greeting the barista at your local coffee shop, or the saleslady at the department store can be counted as progress.

Chapter 6 – Taking It One Step Further

Imagine how challenging it will be to pursue your goals if you do not have enough confidence in yourself. It will become all the more difficult if you do not have a concrete plan to follow, but fear not, because this final chapter will help you flesh out exactly what you want out of life and how you can achieve it confidently.

Define your Focus

We all have that need to accomplish something, but the problem for many is that they do not even know exactly *what* it is that they want to achieve. That is why it is often common and even natural to start off by following the standards of society. Keep in mind that there is nothing wrong with that, especially since some people do find their satisfaction there. However, others feel that something is lacking, therefore, they end up getting frustrated.

Your self-confidence and anyone else's depends heavily on what you consider as your main goal in life. By dedicating all your time and energy towards the one thing that you wish to accomplish, your feelings of self-assurance and confidence will grow.

Of course, you have to know what it is that you want to achieve. In other words, your goal has to be specific, detailed and clear beyond a doubt. However, if you still struggle to define what it is that you want to focus on, then you may want to give the following exercise a try.

This exercise is called the "Confidence Pie" (sometimes referred to as the "confidence wheel"). It will help you determine which aspect of your life you can draw the most confidence from:

Step 1: On a sheet of paper, write down all the different aspects of your life that you believe require you to be confident.

Try to have about six to eight aspects, including family life, career, parenthood, social relationships, academic life, and so on

Step 2: With a scale of 1 to 10 in mind, 10 being the ideal level of confidence you want to have, rate how you feel next to each aspect of your life.

Go with your gut feeling. If you think you are highly confident in your successful career, go ahead and give yourself a 9 or 10. If you think you constantly struggle with dating or social relationships, there is no shame in giving yourself a 2 or 3.

Step 3: On another sheet of paper, draw a big circle to represent your pie. "Slice" your pie into equally sized pieces, each of which represents the aspects of your life you have listed. Label each piece accordingly.

Step 4: Now, fill out each slice of the pie based on their score.

For example, if you gave "career" a score of 9, then 9/10s of the slice should be shaded. If you gave "social relationships" a 2, then shade only 2/10s, and so on. You may use different colored pens to make each pie stand out.

Step 5: Take a good look at the visual representation of your "life" in terms of your confidence level then consider what you can do to make all the slices equal.

Keep the confidence pie in your journal and use it to remind you of the aspects in your life you need to focus on. It is a useful reference to have as you proceed with the next section, which is about goal setting.

Turn your Dreams into Goals

How does it feel to see your own confidence pie? Hopefully, it inspires you to appreciate and develop the different aspects of your life. You may even be eager to get started. To transform yourself into becoming more confident, learn to create goals in an effective and efficient way. One of the best strategies to do that is called the *SMART* model.

This model is an acronym, which you can use to guide you in turning ideas into goals. Here is a breakdown of the model:

- **S: Specific.**

    Your goal needs to be as specific as possible. It is the only way for you to become truly motivated to achieve it.

    For example, if the financial aspect of your life is where you lack confidence, then be detailed about it. Do you want to be more financially secure? How much money do you think will make you feel that way? Your response should not just be "Oh, a lot of money," but "five million dollars" (or more, of course).

    Next, transform this specific goal into something tangible. For instance, you can even write down the figure on a check to yourself then pin it on your corkboard. This will remind you of your specific goal.

- **M: Measurable.**

No matter how specific your goal is, you will not get anywhere if you cannot measure your progress towards it.

For instance, the five million dollar example is quite easy to measure because money is as countable as it can get.

However, let's say you need to improve your confidence in the social relationship aspect of your life. Consider how it should be measured.

Would it be in the form of time, such as by spending one day per week with good friends? Or would you measure it in terms of quality, such as improving your listening skills so that you can have a better conversation with your friend?

- **A: Attainable.**

  There is nothing wrong with a challenging goal, but you also have to make sure that it is realistic. In most cases, you can measure whether your goal is attainable or not by writing down detailed steps that will take you closer to your goal.

For example, if your goal were to acquire five million dollars to feel financially secure and more confident, then think about how you are going to acquire that in a realistic (and honest) way. You can start off by paying off all your debts while exerting an effort to reduce your spending. The next step is to increase your income while also maintaining a modest lifestyle. You can then move on to savings and investments, and so on.

- **R: Relevant.**

  You can only be motivated by a goal that you feel is relevant. In other words, you must be able to answer "why" you want that goal in the first place. Your answer should be something, which gets you pumped up. It is highly important to remind yourself each day of your "why" because you will continue to work towards your goal no matter how challenging the path may be.

  For example, if your goal is to lose weight, ask yourself why you will feel confident once you have achieved it. No matter how simple or how deep your answer to that may be, what matters is that it is rewarding enough to inspire you to commit.

- **T: Timed.**

  The biggest difference between a dream – no matter how specific, measurable, attainable, and rewarding it may be – a goal is the deadline. Without one, you will *always* put off your goal to tomorrow.

However, by setting a deadline, you are racing against the clock to achieve what you want and gain the confidence that you have always wished for.

Now that you have your goals, the next step is to take action. Here are the steps that you can take to achieve your goals:

Step 1: Choose one aspect that you want to focus on.

While there may be several aspects in your life wherein you want to feel more confident, it helps to focus on improving them one at a time. That way, you will not feel overwhelmed.

Once you notice yourself improving in one aspect, you can then move on to focusing on the next one. It helps to start with the aspect that you value the most.

Step 2: Create a statement out of your focus to turn it into a goal.

Use the *SMART* model as your guide.

Step 3: Construct a detailed plan, which will guide you into taking action.

It can be a step-by-step plan, a timeline, or a checklist. Polish your plan until you feel confident in it.

Step 4: Take note of your progress as well as any setbacks. Make adjustments where necessary.

Keep in mind that your detailed plan should not be set in stone. Rather, it should allow you to adapt to unexpected changes. Believe in your goal and you can gain the confidence to roll with the punches.

Step 5: Continue to make progress and adjust to changes.

Think of failures as opportunities to pivot to a different direction. Soon enough, you can find the right path that will lead you to your goal.

Find a Confidence Mentor

Believe it or not, confidence can be contagious. When you surround yourself with people who are confident and help others believe in themselves, it is only natural for you to emulate them. On the other hand, constantly spending time with negative people will also cause you to be more critical of yourself and others.

While it is easy to say that you should choose friends who uplift you and help you find confidence in yourself, not all of us have the luxury to find these people in our life. If you are still working towards being confident enough to meet new people, then the best way to be inspired by others is to find a mentor.

For instance, he or she can be a public figure you admire who regularly posts video blogs on YouTube or who writes uplifting articles online. Aside from regularly getting updates from these mentors, you can also read autobiographies of people who were able to achieve great things despite adversity. Find the time each day, even for just five minutes, to read, listen to or watch someone who motivates you.

How to be the Main Character in your Life

In the movie *The Holiday* (2006), an insecure, troubled character named Iris (played by Kate Winslet) met a retired but wonderfully clever Hollywood director named Arthur (played by Eli Wallach). When she started telling him about how she was still in love with her ex-boyfriend even though he is already engaged to another, he gave her some good advice.

He said, "Iris, in the movies we have leading ladies and we have the best friend. You, I can tell, are a leading lady, but for some reason you are behaving like the best friend."

A lot of people go through life without setting healthy personal standards on themselves. They end up becoming the bit character *in their own life* when in fact they deserve to be just as exceptional, brave, admirable and clever as the lead character. While it goes without saying that real life isn't like the movies, it does not mean you should hold yourself back from being "The One" who saves the day.

How do you gain the confidence to turn yourself into the main character of your own life? Here is what you are going to do:

Step 1: Choose to change for the better. You are in charge of your life, not your family, friends or your boss.

Know that in this world, you are going to be your constant companion. While there is no denying that your relationships are important, your own thoughts, behaviors and choices are all you really have. As soon as you decide to take responsibility for yourself, you will notice a big change in perspective.

Step 2: Verbally state exactly what you want to achieve in life.

Whatever goal it is you have in mind, say it out loud to yourself. You are declaring to yourself and the universe that you are going on a journey towards a goal. This goal will make you feel that you have lived a great life on this earth.

Step 3: Take action!

Arm yourself with a concrete plan and work with what you have. Learn from each day, keeping in mind that mistakes and failures are among the best teachers. Cherish and gain support from good friends. Gain insights from your mentors. Most importantly, don't take the present moment for granted because you can never take time back once it has passed.

Know what you want and become the leader of your own voyage towards achieving your goals. Spend time each day to motivate yourself and stay on the right track. Most importantly, have fun with it. By focusing and taking action on what you truly value in life, confidence will soon follow.

Chapter 7 – You are What You Repeatedly Do

Building self-confidence is a lot like growing a delicate rose from a seedling. It doesn't happen overnight and requires everyday patience, care and attention. The good news is it gets easier with each passing day, and the key is to nurture the right habits. Here are some of the most important habits to start:

Wake up fresh, invigorated and ready to take on the world

This scene may sound like a TV commercial, but waking up bright and early will help you maintain that can-do attitude for the rest of the day. There is a huge difference between struggling to wake up and having that battle with your alarm clock, and waking up nice and easy even before your alarm goes off.

Waking up to an early morning offers you the opportunity to reflect, relax and plan ahead. It also allows you to take charge of the day, instead of letting your schedule overwhelm you. It also helps you know that willpower is at its highest point at the start of the day, then it slowly breaks down with each passing hour. This makes mornings the perfect time to work on the most important tasks of the day.

Following a simple morning routine that you truly enjoy is perhaps the best way to entice you to wake up early. Here are some suggested habits to include in your morning routine that will make you feel inspired and motivated:

- Get your heart rate up through a quick, 20- or even 10-minute exercise. This will instantly make you feel more energized.

- Eat a healthy breakfast. Choosing green tea over a high-sugar morning drink will not only make you feel cleaner and more put-together, but it will also nourish your body better.

- Start grooming immediately. Take an invigorating cold shower. Power-dress, even if you work at home. Do your hair.

- Read or listen to something motivating. A quick, 10- to 15-minute inspirational message from someone you look up to will dramatically improve your outlook for the rest of the day.

- Create or review your list of tasks. It helps to know what you've got planned for the day because this immediately puts things into perspective.

Do an end-of-day Recap

Doing a recap means creating a summary of what transpired during that day. You can either write it down in your journal or you can simply spend 5 or so minutes repeating the recap verbally to yourself. However you choose to do it, it will help you to become more aware of your thoughts and behavior.

That's because self-reflection does wonders to both your cognitive and emotional intelligence. It promotes open-mindedness and curiosity and it helps treat blaming, self-pity, and other negative habits that eat away your confidence.

To do an end-of-day recap, you can ask yourself the following questions:

- How did I feel when I woke up this morning?

- What was the first thing that came into my mind?

- What was my general mood today?

- What made me feel stronger than usual emotions today? Why did I react that way?

- How did I spend my day today?

- Did I feel confident today? Why or why not?

Get in Touch with Nature

No matter where you are in this world, you have access to nature and its wonders. Even those who live in the most bustling metropolises can look up at the sky and gaze at all the distant beings there.

It also reminds you that life is what you make it because whatever choices you make, the seas will continue to make waves and the sky will continue to let clouds pass by. Therefore, finding the time to reconnect with nature will help you realize that you have the power to turn your life around if you so choose.

Here are some simple ideas to help you get in touch with nature:

- Visit the park on a cloudy day and walk barefoot on the grass.

- Go to a nearby beach or lake and soak your toes in the water.

- Gaze up at the sky at night and look at the different patterns of the stars.

- Go on an early morning jog at a nearby woody trail with your friends.

- Observe wild animals in their natural habitat, even if they are just squirrels or birds living in your backyard tree.

Practice Self-Discipline

Just like self-confidence, self-discipline is also a skill that you need to hone. The great thing about improving your self-discipline is that it naturally increases your confidence and improves your self-image at the same time. On the other hand, lacking self-discipline leads to your inability to trust yourself.

If you have been struggling with becoming self-disciplined most of your life, you can start exercising it in the small things. Choose one small habit you want to start, then follow these simple steps to practice self-discipline in it:

Step 1: Set a gentle reminder to help you stay on track.

Step 2: Use an affirmation to motivate you to stick to your commitment.

Step 3: Track your progress in a simple way so that you can see how far you've come along.

Step 4: Reward yourself each time you reach a milestone.

For example, let's say you want to start the habit of waking up early. However, you find it difficult because you tend to go to bed late at night.

In this case, you can start practicing self-discipline by following a regular bedtime schedule. You can set an alarm with a gentle tone on your phone to signal you that it is time for bed. You can even use an affirmation, such as "I love going to bed early" or "My body deserves to rest and enjoy deep sleep."

To track your progress, you can put a stamp on your calendar in each morning after you went to bed on time. Every time you hit a milestone, say going to bed at the prescribed time for twelve consecutive nights, you can reward yourself by having breakfast at your favorite café.

While there are plenty of other confidence-boosting habits to start, these will serve as the foundation of all your other endeavors. Feel free to get creative and infuse your own personality into each of these habits. That way, it becomes effortless to stick with them.

Conclusion

If you are reading this, I truly want to thank you from the bottom of my heart for reading this book.

I hope it was able to help you to gain confidence in yourself and be inspired you to reach out for your goals.

The next step is to take massive action.

Commit to a healthy lifestyle, which promotes a positive outlook on life. Find the time to take good care of yourself. After all, you deserve to be confident and to have all the benefits that come with it. Your confidence will guide you to take actions that are more aligned with your value and to listen to your heart. Continue to surround yourself with people and things that inspire you to do better each day. Let go of whatever is holding you back from feeling strong and confident. Treat others with respect and kindness as well, and don't hesitate to spend quality time with those you love.

Most importantly, never forget that you are just as capable of achieving great things as anyone else. The secret is always to believe in yourself and to never give up.

Thank you and I truly hope that you are going to commit to make your life a masterpiece because the world needs more of the greatness that is inside you!